Hope
Beyond Your Tears

Hope

Beyond Your Tears

Experiencing Christ's Healing Love

Trevor Hudson

Foreword by Dallas Willard

UPPER ROOM BOOKS®
NASHVILLE

The Upper Room Web site: www.upperroom.org

UPPER ROOM®, UPPER ROOM BOOKS®, and design logos are trademarks owned by The Upper Room®, a ministry of GBOD®, Nashville, Tennessee. All rights reserved.

Unless otherwise indicated, scripture quotations are taken from the Holy Bible, New International Version®, NIV®. Copyright © 1973, 1978, 1984, 2011 by Biblica, Inc.™ Used by permission of Zondervan. All rights reserved worldwide. www.zondervan.com

Cover image: iStockphoto/Thinkstock
Cover and interior design: Nancy Terzian, BuckinghorseDesign.com

Library of Congress Cataloging-in-Publication Data
Hudson, Trevor, 1951–
  Hope beyond your tears : experiencing Christ's healing love / by Trevor Hudson.
    p. cm.
  Rev. ed. of: Touched by resurrection love.
  ISBN 978-0-8358-1115-6 (print) — ISBN 978-0-8358-1124-8 (mobi) — ISBN 978-0-8358-1173-6 (epub)
1. Consolation. 2. Suffering—Religious aspects—Christianity. 3. Hope—Religious aspects—Christianity. I. Hudson, Trevor, 1951– Touched by resurrection love. II. Title.
  BV4905.3.H83 2012
  248.8'6—dc23

                                    2012023883

Printed in the United States of America

CONTENTS

FOREWORD

Trevor Hudson is remarkably gifted at unrolling the contents of a scriptural story right into the midst of your life. He is an open soul—something learned through a long spiritual process in his life—who is able to open other souls. Yours and mine. This is our profound need: for our souls to be opened. To turn loose the inner bondages by which we shut ourselves in, away from others and from God. We have been hurt. There we think we are safe. There we die alone. Who can help us?

The opening of a soul comes through little cracks and progresses slowly. We are such beings as can only let go of our inner hold in response to grace—true gift, no strings. Grace gently suggests to us that good is present and coming toward us. This is perceived through a tiny crack in our armor. Could we widen that crack just a bit, get a slightly better view? Perhaps begin to let the gift enter our shell, just a little? Perhaps we could begin by spending some time quietly resting in solitude and silence.

The stories of Jesus are the primary overtures of grace in a world that knows little of true gift. We can let them in. Indeed, they are so winsome, who can keep them out once they appear? They are like raindrops and sunshine, and the flowers in our soul begin to grow. Without our knowing how, without our even intending it. We begin to find good we did not expect or hope for: here, there, in the world, in others. In ourselves, can it be? We ask, "Who has done this?" And we find that Jesus himself came in with the stories. Meditation is turning to the gift of Jesus. Waiting before it. Paying attention. Letting things be what they are. Finding we have a soul. Suspecting that we are an unceasing spiritual being with an eternal destiny in the world of a good God. Meditation itself proves to be a gift in retrospect. At first Mary "did not know it was Jesus." Thought he was the gardener! What we learn in meditation upon Christ is from another world but does not demand understanding at the outset, just longing from the heart. Mary had that. You probably do too. So make space for it and take this book as a guide. Just follow the instructions given by the author. Let the words wash over you. They will do the work. You can count on it.

Dallas Willard

INTRODUCTION

For nearly four decades I have worked as a pastor in a local congregation. It has been a huge privilege. These years have made me deeply aware of the depth and extent of human trauma, bereavement, anxiety, and emotional pain that lies all around us and also in our hearts. Nearly everyone carries a heavy burden. Perhaps you do too. If you do, I would like to offer you these meditations on one of my favorite Easter stories—the encounter between the risen Christ and Mary Magdalene.

It is a deeply moving story of the transformation and hope that can lie beyond our tears. It begins with Mary, brokenhearted and weeping, standing outside the tomb where Jesus had been buried after his crucifixion. Her whole world has collapsed. But her story does not end here. It closes with her running to find the other disciples to report the incredible news that Christ was alive. Her darkest night had suddenly been changed into brightest day. She had experienced the transforming power of the resurrection for herself. She had become a person of Easter faith living in a Good Friday world.

This transforming experience has become a reality for countless people throughout the centuries and still happens today. The risen Christ continues to meet with us at the point of our deepest need. As he came to Mary two-thousand years ago, so he comes to us in our dark and difficult places. Sometimes, like Mary herself, we do not recognize Jesus immediately. But as we open our hearts and our minds to his living presence and to the message of his resurrection, we find ourselves gradually empowered to live beyond our tears, to go out and connect with those suffering around us.

Another reason for writing this book has been to encourage others to really live in a Gospel story. It becomes too easy to turn Bible reading into a mere intellectual exercise, which can happen whenever we read the Bible without being touched and transformed by what we read. We gain more information, but we remain the same. Through these meditations I want to show you how to stay with a Gospel story for a few weeks and allow it to permeate your entire life. When you do this, you will experience the resurrection power of the Christian message to overcome sorrow with joy, darkness with light, and defeat with victory.

As you read this book, I encourage you to do so meditatively. I suggest that you take a few days to read each chapter, allowing five to ten minutes after each reading to reflect on what you've read. You may wish to ask yourself, *What thoughts crossed my mind, and what feelings did I experience as I read this chapter?* Take the time to record your reflections.

It would be even better to read this book with one or two friends or in a small group. Each week group members could get together, share their reflections, and learn from one another's experiences. Our journey in faith is always a journey together. I have also offered three questions at the end of each chapter that will help you to relate better to what you have read, along with a prayer that you can use each day. I have called this prayer a "breath prayer" because I hope that praying it will become second nature to you.

Let me end this introduction by offering you a prayer that you might like to pray before beginning this book. This prayer was written by a dear friend whose life represented a living expression of the Resurrection. His resurrection faith helped him to overcome a terrible depression, to live through the death of one of his children, and to shape his life into a powerful channel of God's love and care.

Here is the prayer:

> I ask you, life-giving and victorious, resurrected Jesus, to help me grasp the full meaning of your victory over suffering, death, and evil; and to help me live with hope and love, with joy and expectation, with patience and determination, and with confidence and peace as I prepare for the transcendent fellowship of eternity that you have opened to me by your death and resurrection. May I now know something of the kingdom for which you told me to pray and then know its fullness by growing forever in your loving presence.
>
> — *Morton Kelsey*

May these meditations open your heart and mind to be touched by resurrection love.

Chapter 1

BEFRIENDING OUR TEARS

Mary stood outside the tomb crying. As she wept, she bent over to look into the tomb and saw two angels in white, seated where Jesus' body had been, one at the head and the other at the foot.

—John 20:11–12

It was the late seventies, and I was sitting with Gordon Cosby, cofounder and pastor of the Church of the Saviour, a small, vibrant, ecumenical congregation in the inner city of Washington, D.C. We were having lunch in the Potter's House, one of the church's many ministries serving the city, and reflecting on the challenges of preaching within the contemporary urban context. Almost forty years of servant ministry had given my lunch companion a profound pastoral wisdom. When I asked him whether he had anything to say to me about sharing the gospel on the suffering continent of Africa, he responded, "Always remember that each person you see in the congregation sits next to his or her own pool of tears."

I have never forgotten these words. Nearly every time I stand to share the good news from God with others, this sentence comes into my mind. The words always remind me of the suffering present among those gathered together.

Always remember that each person you see in the congregation sits next to his or her own pool of tears.

This knowledge creates a difficult awareness from which to preach and teach. At times I am deeply concerned that my words will come across as glib or superficial or perhaps even empty. As I write this meditation, I am aware of these possibilities. Certainly Gordon's words to me have increased my discomfort with any kind of spiritual talk that overlooks the pain that people experience.

Each of us does sit next to a pool of tears. As you read my words you are sitting beside your pool; and as I write these words, I am seated next to mine. Our pools are different. Some are deeper; some are muddier. Some have been caused by what has been done to us; some are the result of our own doing. These pools remind us of the grief and losses that we have experienced through our lives. It might have been the death of a loved one, the pain of divorce, abuse as a child, the unmet longing for a partner, the loss of a job, or a rejection by a close friend. There are many different kinds of pools—the list goes on and on.

But tears don't have to end in sadness and pain. As different as our pools of tears may be, they can lead us into a new space of change and growth. If we allow our tears to tell their stories, they can become the means by which our lives are transformed. Whether they flow down our cheeks or represent our cries for help—the silent needs of our grieving and broken hearts—our tears have the potential to become the agents of resurrection and newness. We learn this truth when we think more deeply about the encounter between the risen Jesus and Mary Magdalene on that first Easter morning.

Let us begin to explore this meeting, this story about the journey to transformation that lies beyond tears. When we find Mary standing outside the tomb, she is weeping. Two days earlier, she had seen the person whom

Whether they flow down our cheeks or represent our cries for help—the silent needs of our grieving and broken hearts— our tears have the potential to become the agents of resurrection and newness.

she loved dearly, the one who had released her from her torment, put to death on a cross. No doubt his death had left her confused, numb, and desperate. Ever since the initial encounter when Jesus had freed her (Luke 8:2), her whole life had revolved around him. The Gospel accounts bear witness to the fact that she had followed him around Galilee. She had been at the foot of the cross. She had accompanied his crucified body to the tomb in Joseph's garden. Then, early on Sunday morning, she had gone with a small group of women to the tomb. To their great distress, they found the stone rolled away and the body of Jesus gone. Soon afterward Peter and John arrived, only to depart and leave Mary alone in the garden, standing beside her pool of tears.

The longer I think about Mary's tears, the more I recognize the need for her to cry. She needed those tears to express the deep grief of her heart. They were necessary to ease the intensity of her inner pain. They were necessary to relax those raw nerves rapidly reaching the breaking point. They were necessary to lighten the weight of sorrow bearing heavily down upon her spirit. They were necessary for the processes of healing and transformation to begin. Indeed, I believe that without her tears, Mary may have failed to recognize the shining figures inside the tomb. After all, tears can help us to see things differently. They clear the dust from our eyes and give us fresh insight and vision.

Mary's tears also remind us that crying is part of being human. Some of us, especially men, need this reminder. Often we feel uncomfortable about our tears. Over the years I have attended many funerals where I witnessed heartbroken mourners struggling to hold back their tears, almost as if those tears were not appropriate. Earlier today I sat with a young man in his midthirties,

After all, tears can help us to see things differently. They clear the dust from our eyes and give us fresh insight and vision.

who, as he told me the story of his marriage breaking up, began to cry. Reaching for a tissue from the table between us, he apologized.

"I'm sorry for breaking down like this," he said as he blew his nose. "I really need to get a grip on myself."

How different it was for Mary in her personal pain and grief—she seemed to know that tears were an intimate part of what it means to be a human being in pain. We need to learn from her.

Today I invite you to glimpse the promise hidden in your pool of tears. Those tears hold the promise of new beginnings. One way to do this would be to become quiet for a few moments and imaginatively join Mary as she stands weeping outside the tomb. Envision yourself meeting Mary in the garden, her eyes and yours filled with tears. Go together across to the open tomb, look inside, and slowly take in what you see. Witness the intriguing emptiness of the grave . . . the grave clothes neatly folded . . . the shroud and napkin lying separately.

Now stand for a moment at your own pool of tears and reflect on it in the light of this resurrection picture. Weep if you need to. Allow this Easter-morning scene to deepen your belief that, on the other side of your brokenness, grief, and loss lie the possibilities of new beginnings. We can look at our tears and give up in anguish and despair, or we can look up to God through them and hope for transformation. I encourage you to make the second choice. Resurrection life and tears often interweave, which could be why the psalmist, many centuries ago, celebrated the promise that "those who sow with tears will reap with songs of joy."

Memory Verse

Those who sow with tears
will reap with songs of joy.
                    —Psalm 126:5

Breath Prayer

Lord, fill my life with resurrection hope.

Time to Reflect

Describe the thoughts and feelings you experienced while reading this chapter.

Taking It Further in Group Sharing

- In what ways can you identify with Mary as she stands weeping outside the tomb?

- What would it mean for you to look up to God through your tears and hope for new beginnings?

- How does the message of Jesus' death and resurrection help you to befriend your tears?

Chapter 2

PROCESSING PAIN

Jesus said to Mary, "Woman, why are you crying?"
—John 20:15

One moment in my journey through tears to transformation stands out clearly in my memory. It was 1981, and I had just started an appointment in a new congregation. Obviously keen to do well, I was working ten to twelve hours a day, neglecting to care for myself and often unavailable to Debbie, my new partner in marriage. Not surprisingly, I began struggling with a nagging depression that I could not overcome.

One weekend during this period, I was the speaker at a large youth conference. After I had finished my first talk, I came down from the stage and headed for the canteen to buy a cool drink. On my way a colleague, who worked as a psychiatrist and lecturer on the staff of a major medical school, came over and said quietly that if I ever needed to talk to someone, he would be available.

To this day, I do not know what prompted him to extend that caring invitation. I can only guess that my colleague discerned the hidden cry in my heart. Nonetheless, his invitation gave me the courage to phone the following week and make an appointment to see him.

I remember clearly our first time together, on a bitterly cold September day. We met in a counseling room at a children's hospital near Johannesburg's city center. He had graciously offered to see me at seven o'clock, before his working day began. As soon as I sat down I began to sob uncontrollably. I sobbed for almost half an hour. When my crying began to subside, my companion gently asked, "Trevor, can you tell me the story that lies behind your tears?"

Looking back, I can see more clearly the importance of that question. Our tears always need to be carefully examined. Sometimes they can be sentimental or manipulative or even self-indulgent. Some of us just cry easily. My companion's question invited me to trace the source of my tears, to explore where they were coming from. As I started to talk, I began a personal journey through tears to transformation—a journey that continues to this present day. I was reminded of the onset of this journey recently when I dug out my journal and read again what I had written about that meeting.

> **24-09-81** I saw Cliff yesterday for the first time. It was an intensely painful time. I felt a physical pain in my body that I have not felt before. There were many tears. I don't know where they came from. But it was good to speak. As I heard my own words, I understood a little more why I feel so much pain. It's the painful thought that if I cannot do anything for anybody, I will not be acceptable to others. I wonder where this thought comes from. We made another appointment, and it seems as if our relationship is going to continue.

My friend's question to me was similar to the one that came to Mary, first from the angels inside the tomb and then from Jesus standing behind her. Their question was, "Woman, why are you crying?" Notice that this question suggests neither judgment nor condemnation. And Jesus did not say, "Mary, why don't you put an end to your tears?

Can't you see it is Easter morning? Pull yourself together and get on with your life." Rather, their question invites Mary to give voice to her pain, to bring to speech what she is experiencing, to share the story behind her tears. This question communicates profound respect, deep interest, and warm concern. And Mary feels safe enough to

Pain must be processed if it is to become a positive, constructive experience.

respond, "They have taken my Lord away. . . and I don't know where they have put him" (John 20:13).

Like Mary, we need to hear that same question personally addressed to us so that we may offer our own personal response. To avoid this question is to avoid our pain, and the consequences of running away from our personal pain can be both numerous and harmful. They can range from persistent depression, irrational outbursts of anger, and spiritual desolation, to having difficulty in ministering to others who are experiencing pain. Pain must be processed if it is to become a positive, constructive experience. Pain needs to find a voice and be expressed. One way to accomplish this is to share the story behind our tears. When we do, we begin that sacred journey that leads us through our tears to transformation.

I don't think our pools of tears will ever totally dry up this side of the grave. They may alter in size or shape or change in depth, but they seldom go away completely. However, we must not give up hope.

Taking time to find someone we trust to be our "wailing wall" and sharing the stories that our tears represent brings immense healing benefits into our lives and relationships. Something positive and life-giving is released when our tears flow and find their voice. This could be why the church, long before the advent of modern psychology, gave special attention to "the gift of tears." Besides their therapeutic value, which is well documented, tears help us realize when we have reached the point when we are most wounded, which is precisely the moment that restorative grace and new beginnings often enter our lives. Our tears make us receptive to angelic presences and surprising resurrection encounters. It happened for Mary, and it can happen for us as well.

You may find it helpful right now, as you are reading these words, to respond to the question that came to Mary on that first Easter morning. "Why are you crying?" In a simple prayer sentence offer your response:

- "Lord, I'm crying today because I'm grieving."

- "Lord, I'm crying today because my marriage is in pain."

- "Lord, I'm crying today because I feel as if I'm completely in the dark."

- "Lord, I'm crying today because I don't know which way to turn."

- "Lord, I'm crying today because I am far from you."

- "Lord, I'm crying today because I can't seem to find you anywhere."

Whatever your response may be, sharing your story about this question, both with the risen Lord and with a trusted listener or small group, could open the way for you to begin your journey through tears to transformation. Through such sharing you come to realize that you are not alone. You are connected not only with the God who weeps with you but also with other hurting and fragile human beings. When we become aware of our connections with God and with one another, we receive the strength and courage to live creatively, even in the midst of our pain. This is my prayer for you as you read these words.

Memory Verse

Hear my cry, O God;
listen to my prayer.
                    —Psalm 61:1

Breath Prayer

Lord, thank you for listening when I pour out my pain.

Time to Reflect

Describe the thoughts and feelings you experienced while reading this chapter.

Taking It Further in Group Sharing

- Describe a time in your life when someone was there for you in a time of struggle and pain.

- What did this person teach you about being a wailing wall for others?

- What or who helps you to process pain in your life?

Chapter 3

WEEPING WITH THOSE WHO WEEP

Rejoice with those who rejoice; mourn with those who mourn.

—Romans 12:15

The encounter between Jesus and Mary Magdalene reminds us to take seriously one crucial New Testament ministry—the ministry of weeping with those who weep. This is important. We can become so absorbed in our own pain and the stories behind it that we do not see the tears of those around us. We forget that the risen Christ, who meets us in our tears, calls us to embody his presence in a deeply wounded world. He calls us always to follow him to those places where people are struggling and in need and to share in his ministry of wiping away their tears. One way to accomplish this task is to weep with those who weep.

How, you may be wondering, *can we do this?* The answer is simple but not easy to implement. We begin by learning from Jesus. What would Jesus do if he were

❧

As we go about learning these ways
of weeping with those who weep, we
participate in the resurrection practice of
wiping away the tears of others.

❧

in our place? We watch him take the initiative and reach out to Mary in her tears. We listen as he asks her to put her weeping into words. We observe as he listens without judgment or condemnation to the story she shares. Then, in dependence on his Spirit, we learn how to follow in his footsteps as we meet and interact with those who suffer in our midst: how to take the first step in getting closer to others in their pain, how to ask those questions that will help them to discover the voice of their tears, how to listen with respectful attention and interest to what they say. As we go about learning these ways of weeping with those who weep, we participate in the resurrection practice of wiping away the tears of others.

I witnessed this type of resurrection practice a few weeks ago. I was preaching in a church in Cape Town and noticed a man crying. After the service I saw one of the local leaders, an internationally recognized author and theologian, go across the sanctuary and speak to the weeping man. I joined the rest of the congregation in another room for refreshments. When I returned to the sanctuary about an hour later to fetch my Bible and sermon notes, the two men were still sitting together, the one listening intently and the other speaking. From a distance I could see that the first man had stopped crying.

Later that day I had lunch with the leader and his family. I asked him about his encounter after the church service.

"What happened between you and that crying man?"

"I saw him sitting there weeping; so I went across, sat

with him, and asked if he wanted to speak about it," he answered.

"Where did it go from there?"

"His story just poured out. In all my years of ministry and listening to people, I have seldom come across a story of such intense pain and misery."

"Were you able to be helpful?"

"There was nothing practical I could do," he responded. "But the one thing I asked was whether we could meet again for him to tell me more of his story."

"Do you think that will help?"

"I don't know for sure. But I'm convinced that new life will come when he has been able to tell his story fully to someone who will listen."

This leader was sharing in the ministry of weeping with those who weep. Did you see how similar his actions were to the way in which Jesus reached out to Mary Magdalene in her tears? First of all, the leader was aware enough to look beyond himself. He was not preoccupied with his own needs or with his own group of friends. Second, he took the initiative and approached the person in need. Next, he asked him to share his story of struggle and listened to it. He didn't provide pat answers or offer the person easy solutions. Rather, he gave this desperate person room to speak freely and openly about his pain. And lastly, he assured the man of his ongoing care and concern. Four simple steps, but steps that made it possible for this caring leader to become a wailing wall for someone who needed one.

⟨⊗⟩

We may worship together,
pray together, serve together, and
still be totally unaware of the tears
present in our sister's or brother's heart.

⟨⊗⟩

Ideally, this process demonstrates what the church needs to be like—a community where we can come together, tell our stories, share our pain, and find hope again. If we in the church practiced Jesus' model of sharing, there would be less need for the costly care of secular psychologists. Unfortunately, the sad fact remains that church members are often strangers to one another's pain. We may worship together, pray together, serve together, and still be totally unaware of the tears present in our sister's or brother's heart. The failure to provide room for the sharing of our painful stories is one reason people leave the church and go elsewhere to find healing and transformation for their broken lives. Often these other places provide people an opportunity to share their pain in a climate of acceptance and warmth that cannot be found in the church.

❦

Community develops not only as we share our joys but also as we share our pain.

❦

Perhaps, beginning with your and my combined efforts, this situation could right itself. From today onward we can resolve to become more aware of those around us who are living in pain. Almost every day people come knocking on the doors of our lives, hoping for an ear that will listen. It might be a colleague at work, a team member at the club, or a brother or sister in the faith. It may even be someone with whom we live. We are called simply to be there, to take a caring interest, and to listen to the story behind the person's tears. Paul did not advise his churches to "cheer up those who weep"; he said "weep with those who weep." In other words, enter as deeply as you can into the grief and pain of your neighbor. We cannot take on the suffering of the whole world, but we can reach out to those near us who need us most.

As critical and effective as this one-to-one ministry can be, however, I believe we are called to take a further step. We need to create simple structures in our larger groups and congregations that facilitate sharing our personal stories, especially the painful ones. One night a week, a small group to which I belong tries to provide this sort of climate. Our group consists of five families, all with teenage and young children, and all at very different stages on the Christian path. We often begin our evening with an invitation to "share a joy or sorrow from the past week." I am continually struck by the ways this simple question facilitates storytelling and story sharing. Community develops not only as we share our joys but also as we share our pain. If you belong to a small group, experiment by making this question a regular part of its agenda. Do not be surprised if the risen Christ meets with your group in a special way.

Learning to weep with those who weep is a life-long journey. I hope that this meditation has given you a glimpse of how you can share in this ministry. We must move beyond the concept of processing our personal pain to the place where we can reach out to others around us who are in pain. We can do this in our personal relationships. And we can create those types of safe and sacred spaces in our faith communities where people can share the stories that lie behind their tears. If we rise to this challenge, we become Easter people in a Good Friday world.

Memory Verse

Carry each other's burdens, and in this way you will fulfill the law of Christ.

—Galatians 6:2

Breath Prayer

Lord, help me to connect today with someone in pain.

Time to Reflect

Describe the thoughts and feelings you experienced while reading this chapter.

Taking It Further in Group Sharing

- Share one experience where you felt God used you to "weep with those who weep."

- What was this experience like for you? (Be careful not to mention the names of the people involved.)

- What human cry in your surrounding community moves you most deeply at the moment?

Chapter 4

EXPERIENCING
RESURRECTION LOVE

Jesus said to her, "Mary."

—John 20:16

More than any other spiritual leader in South Africa, Archbishop emeritus Desmond Tutu has constantly worked within the public arena to affirm the good news that God loves each one of us. A South African newspaper published an interview with Archbishop Tutu written by a journalist from the British newspaper *The Telegraph*. The journalist had traveled to South Africa to get an Easter message for the overseas public. As they sat together around the dining room table in the Tutu home,

Desmond spoke about his struggle with prostate cancer, his views about the afterlife, and his relationship with God. As the interview came to an end, the journalist reported that the Archbishop abandoned the role of the one being interviewed and became instead a witness to resurrection love. Archbishop Tutu, sensing that the reporter was a lapsed Anglican, leaned across the table and, in a voice barely above a whisper, said to him:

> "God loves you as you are—with your doubts, with your intellectual reservations, with your inability to make the leap of faith. God says, 'I made you, actually, and I made you as you are because I love you. Don't try to titivate yourself. Just be you and know that I affirm you. You matter enormously to me. You matter as if you were the only human being. And, you know something, I create only masterpieces. I have no doubt at all about your worth. You don't have to do anything. Your worth for me is intrinsic. Please believe that I love you. You are not going to find ultimate satisfaction in anything out there because I made you like me.'"

I'm keenly aware of the difficulty that many people have in accepting personally the validity of the archbishop's words. When they look around, life does not appear to be penetrated by God's resurrection love and grace and mercy. The world seems too full of tragedy and pain to believe that God cares about every human being. They consider the terrible, widespread suffering caused by earthquakes, poverty, drought, crime, injustice, acts of terrorism, and, on a more personal level, illness, grief, cost-cutting, and depression; and they ask, "In the face of all this suffering, how can we believe that a god who calls each one of us by name even exists?"

Perhaps even Mary Magdalene asked this question when she thought about the unfair and unjust events that had taken place on that awful Friday. So let us return to her encounter with Jesus outside the empty tomb, and see how God's personal love came to her.

When Jesus first speaks to Mary as he stands behind her and asks her about her tears, she is unsure who is addressing her. Thinking that he could be the gardener, she answers, "Sir, if you have carried him away, tell me where you have put him, and I will get him." The stranger does not respond, and Mary turns away to face the tomb again. Then she hears a voice simply calling, "Mary."

Immediately Mary recognizes the voice as the same voice that had addressed her with the same gentleness and tenderness at a time when she had become accustomed to hearing scorn and derision. She could never forget that voice! Now as it calls out to her, she cries out, "*Rabboni*," an Aramaic word that means "Teacher."

There are few more powerful scenes in any of the four Gospels. To appreciate just a little of its poignancy, imagine yourself in Mary's place, hearing your name being called by the risen One.

I once invited a small group at a retreat to imagine themselves in Mary's place and then briefly to share their experience. One person responded by saying that it felt too good to be true. Another felt overwhelmed by joy. My personal response was one of sheer wonder and amazement. How do you think you would have responded? Our imagined responses give us a small idea of what it must have been like for Mary to hear her name being called that first Easter morning. Perhaps, if she were asked to describe the significance of the moment, she would have said something like this:

"When I heard my name being called by that familiar voice, I could hardly believe it. But it was true! Jesus, the one who had made me feel like I really mattered as a human being, the one who had given me my life back, was alive. The love that I experienced through his words and actions had not died with the crucifixion. His love was stronger than all the powers of evil and sin and death put together. When this truth dawned on me, it filled me with an incredible sense of joy and hope. I know for sure now that Jesus is my living teacher and friend, my mentor and Lord. I know that there is nothing that could separate me from his love."

Mary's experience invites us into a deeper appreciation of what the Easter message is truly about. It reminds us that at the heart of all things lies a resurrection love that seeks us passionately, calls us by name, and desires a personal relationship with each of us; that the resurrected Jesus and the God whom he reveals know each of us uniquely and individually. When we realize this, as Mary did, everything changes. We do not live, as we may have thought, in a cold, impersonal, and loveless universe. We are not the insignificant and isolated individuals that we sometimes imagine. Rather, we are eternal creatures of infinite worth, living in a universe permeated by brilliant rays of resurrection love and mercy and grace.

I realize that as you read these words you may struggle with the reality of God's personal love. If you do, allow me to make one simple suggestion: take a long look at the risen Jesus as he appeared to Mary. New Testament writers have a powerful belief that if we want to know what God

❦

If you have never known the power of God's love, then maybe it is because you have never asked to know it—I mean really asked, expecting an answer.

❦

is really like, we must look at Jesus (e.g., Luke 10:21-22; John 14:9; Col. 1:15). As you watch Jesus seeking Mary out and calling her by name, imagine that ray of resurrection love piercing Mary's tears of pain and grief. Ask the Spirit of God to help you recognize this resurrection love as it shines toward you. Usually this intimate God-love comes to us in very down-to-earth and ordinary ways—a loving touch, an unexpected call, a meal together, the early morning song of a bird. And if we do not remain alert and aware, we may easily miss it.

I have learned the importance of asking God to help us come to know and experience this resurrection love from personal experience. The assurance that I am personally known, accepted, and loved by God has not come easily to me. But over the years, as I immerse myself in Gospel stories like the one with Mary, I have grasped the importance of asking God to give me an awareness of this love, not only in my head but also in my heart. Frederick Buechner writes, "If you have never known the power of God's love, then maybe it is because you have never asked to know it—I mean really asked, expecting an answer." Almost each day I find myself asking God to open my eyes that I may see the beams of resurrection love around me in the events and experiences of my daily life. By doing this, I have gradually discovered that our belovedness can become an inner knowing that fills our whole lives.

I hope that this meditation will help you to experience the resurrection love that lies at the heart of all things. When you do, everything changes. Your life becomes saturated with wondrous significance. You are known! You are precious! You are accepted! You are deeply loved!

When you experience this good news with your mind and heart, you find yourself taking another step through your tears to transformation. This is the good news that Archbishop Tutu tried to share with the journalist. Certainly this is the message that Mary Magdalene would want to share with you.

Memory Verse

You did not choose me, but I chose you.

—John 15:16

Breath Prayer

Lord, help me to experience your resurrection love today.

Time to Reflect

Describe the thoughts and feelings you experienced while reading this chapter.

Taking It Further in Group Sharing

- How do you respond to the archbishop's words about God's personal love for each one of us?

- Describe a time when God's love touched you in a special way.

- How do you experience God's love in your daily life?

Chapter 5

TURNING AROUND

She turned . . .

—John 20:16

As a young person, I had a very negative understanding of repentance. Whenever someone mentioned the word, a certain picture came into my mind. I remember it clearly—a picture of a somewhat gloomy looking man wearing a long gray overcoat, walking down the street, and holding a sign that read, "Repent, for the end is nigh." To this day I do not know where this mental image came from, but I do know that I did not find this view of repentance inviting. Repentance seemed more a threat than an invitation. Not surprisingly, one of the last things I ever wanted to do was repent.

Over time I came to understand repentance differently. I am thankful for this change, since repentance forms one of the most important themes in the message that Jesus brought. You may remember how, in his first recorded words, he announced, "The time has come. . . . The kingdom of God has come near. . . . Repent and believe the good news!" (Mark 1:15). Quite clearly, Jesus did not consider repentance as something with which to threaten his hearers. Rather, the call to repent was an invitation for

True repentance involves . . . the complete turnaround of our mind and outlook, one that leaves us facing a new direction.

them to enter into a new kind of life, a life permeated by the immediacy of God's presence and peace and power. Repentance, supported by our faith, symbolized that part we are called to play in the drama of our own salvation. What, therefore, does the word *repentance* mean?

In describing Mary's "turning around" to Jesus, the writer of the Gospel of John provides a wonderful word picture of what repentance encompasses. *Repentance* is a translation of the Greek word *metanoia*, which essentially implies a change in our way of thinking, literally a turning back or a turning around. Repentance does not mean putting ourselves down, being preoccupied with our sinfulness, or feeling sorry for ourselves. It may involve feeling remorse for what we have done but is never about earning acceptance, deserving to be forgiven, or trying to win God's favor. True repentance involves something altogether different, the complete turnaround of our mind and outlook, one that leaves us facing a new direction.

Reflect for a few moments on this picture of Mary's "turning moment." To begin with, notice that she turns *in response* to hearing her name being called. God's personal love for you and me always initiates and precedes our repentance. Throughout our lives, indeed right from our beginnings, God constantly seeks us, nudges us, and prompts us into this change of mind and outlook. We do not earn God's love and forgiveness with our repentance or our good deeds. Our "turning around" simply enables us to experience those gifts that God wants to give us—the gifts of acceptance and mercy and new beginnings. The tragedy of not turning is that we miss out on experiencing these life-changing treasures for ourselves.

Next, Mary turns *as she is*, in her grief, pain, and tears. But she turns toward life and a fresh beginning. One of the

⁓

Repentance is a way of life,
a lifelong process of turning in a
Godward direction one day at a time
that keeps our lives open
to the possibilities of
transformation and change.

⁓

central meanings of repentance encompasses turning toward Jesus as we are and accepting the gifts of the kingdom that he freely offers. When we turn (or return) to our Creator, we don't first have to tidy ourselves up and get everything in order. Our trust lies not in our own goodness but in the power of God's personal and intimate love to change us. That old familiar hymn puts it so well, "Just as I am, without one plea . . . O Lamb of God, I come!" As we turn to Christ, our lives become touched by resurrection love; and his work of changing us from the inside begins.

Lastly, be aware that this is *not the first time* that Mary has turned toward Jesus. Many months previously, after he had ministered deeply to her in her brokenness, she had joined the group that followed him. Mary reminds us that repentance is not a once-and-for-all experience. Repentance is a way of life, a lifelong process of turning in a Godward direction one day at a time, which keeps our lives open to the possibilities of transformation and change. It would seem that there are many layers of consciousness within us, and on our journey toward God we constantly discover new pockets of unsurrendered self-centeredness and self-interest. Such discoveries, explains Gerard Hughes, are signs of growth and progress along the spiritual way, not of failure. Christ's invitation to repent is a call to recognize these pockets of sinfulness and to entrust ourselves anew to God's goodness and mercy.

Allow me to share how these interwoven threads of repentance have been present in my own spiritual journey. For the first sixteen years of my life, I had hardly any contact with Christians or the Christian faith. Then, when I was in tenth grade, I met Phillip, a fellow student, who was a follower of Christ. After a short period of friendship, I realized that there was something radically different about Phillip's life. God seemed very real to him, and this divine reality gave Phillip a clear sense of purpose and direction.

Only God can bring about the deep, inner transformation for which our hearts long.

One day I asked him about this. He introduced me to the story of Jesus, explaining especially how Jesus had revealed God's love through his death and resurrection. Phillip told me that if I wanted to experience the transforming love and power of God, I needed to turn toward Christ and ask him to be Lord of my life. Later that night, walking down Havelock Street in Port Elizabeth, I did this on my own by praying a simple prayer of personal commitment and surrender.

That was my *first* "turning moment." But it was certainly not the last. My initial "complete surrender" turned out to be anything but complete. Over the past several decades I have had to turn and return to God, again and again and at many different levels. Nearly every day my feelings and thoughts and actions reveal fresh layers of self-centeredness and self-interest. With the help of supportive mentors and soul friends, I have learned not to berate or punish myself when confronted with these sinful dimensions of my life; instead, I remind myself of the incredible depths of God's resurrection love and entrust myself again to Christ, "warts and all." Only God can bring about the deep, inner transformation for which our hearts long.

I invite you to spend a few moments now thinking about your own journey of repentance. Begin by recalling the circumstances in which you first turned toward God. Remember where you were living, what you were doing, and how God's love first came to you. Was your turning a sudden or a gradual experience? Were there friends or family members who helped you turn? And since that moment, how have you continued to travel along the road of repentance? When have you experienced other critical moments of turning? How do you sense God nudging you at the moment into a deeper surrender of yourself? It would be exciting if, as you finish reading this meditation, you entered into a deepened experience of repentance. It could open your life to a renewed experience of resurrection life.

Memory Verse

[Do you not realize] that God's kindness is intended to lead you to repentance?

—Romans 2:4

Breath Prayer

Lord, help me to turn and yield myself to you afresh.

Time to Reflect

Describe the thoughts and feelings you experienced while reading this chapter.

Taking It Further in Group Sharing

- Describe your first "turning moment."

- How do you experience God in your turning moments?

- In what ways do you sense God nudging you into a deeper repentance?

Chapter 6

BECOMING A LEARNER
OF JESUS

She turned toward him and cried out in Aramaic,
"Rabboni!" (which means "Teacher").

—John 20:16

Recently, I undertook some further studies. Becoming a student again in my fifties presented quite a challenge. Nonetheless, it proved to be a time of new learning and expanding my horizons. One of the things that being a student again clarified for me was how so much of our knowledge about life comes from other people. Whether it be from our parents, our schoolteachers, our pastors, our peers, our bosses at work, or our favorite television personality, throughout our lives we are constantly learning from others how to live. Even when we claim that we make up our own minds, we often have done so because someone suggested a certain course of action or opinion to us. In a nutshell, we are always someone's disciple to some degree or another.

❧

When we turn toward Christ, we do well to come as learners.

❧

One of the most revealing moments in our lives occurs when we begin to reflect on who our most significant teachers have been and to critically examine the effects that their words, opinions, and actions have exerted on our lives. If these effects have been life-giving and creative, we have a great deal to give thanks for. Sadly, sometimes the ideas about life that we have gleaned from others may not have worked in our favor or may even have done much damage and caused considerable heartache. The good news, however, lies in the fact that the process of learning how to live never ends. We can always choose again whose disciple we want to be.

Mary Magdalene was clear about whose disciple she wanted to be. When she turned toward Jesus, she called out, "Teacher!" By using this word she gave us a glimpse of what her relationship with Jesus meant to her. Besides being her dearest friend and life-giving deliverer, Jesus was also her beloved "rabbi" whose words had illuminated her life. He had helped her to make sense of her world and had given her new purpose and direction. His teachings had shown her how to build her life upon a rock. Now his victory over death gave eternal validity to his words and example. By raising him from the grave, God had underlined Jesus' teachings with divine authority. Whatever the future of her relationship with Jesus would become, Mary somehow wanted to remain a learner in the company of Jesus. She instinctively expressed this deep desire with her exclamation, "Teacher!"

In this word Mary reminds us that when we turn toward Christ we do well to come as learners. After all, our repentance makes us citizens of a radically different new kingdom, a kingdom where the last are first, the weak are strong, and the leaders are servants first. We will want to learn all we can about this strange kingdom and how we can participate in it. We encounter a new language to learn—the language of self-giving and sacrificial love—and a family history to make our own, a history of God's people that stretches from biblical times into the present. There

We need to let Christ, our living teacher, transform us from within, changing our habits and automatic responses in the reality of this present world.

are new habits to adopt—habits of worship and prayer, life sharing and servanthood, giving and receiving. Following Jesus as learners ushers us into this different kingdom, opens our hearts to the power of the Spirit, and gradually transforms our character into God's family likeness.

How, then, do you and I become learners of Jesus? Obviously it cannot mean trying to become carbon copies of his Palestinian life, with its sandals and robes. It would not make sense for us to try to live the kind of life Jesus lived two thousand years ago. Consider some of the differences between our lives and his. Jesus was not married, did not have children, didn't drive to work on congested highways each morning, and was not faced with the particular challenges with which we contend today. There is just no way in which we can or should try to copy Jesus' historical lifestyle. We cannot uproot ourselves from our present lives as spouses, parents, and highway commuters, or separate ourselves from a world of high technology and social complexity in order to imitate Jesus in his cultural and social setting.

Nor, I dare suggest, does being a disciple of Jesus mean constantly asking ourselves, "What would Jesus do [WWJD] in my present situation?" There is nothing wrong with asking the WWJD question. But in many cases we already know what Jesus would do. The problem arises because, regardless of what we think Jesus would do, we often end up doing what our nature and our habits have trained us to do. In other words, what lives "in us" instinctively comes out. The crucial challenge facing us, therefore, involves learning from Jesus how to transform our inner selves and become the kind of people who naturally and habitually embody how he would respond to any given situation. To put it simply, we need to let Christ, our living teacher, transform us from within, thereby changing our habits and automatic responses in the reality of this present world.

This inner transformation of the "command center" of our being happens as we embark on a learning journey with rabbi Jesus, who remains alive and present in our midst. We ask the ever-living Christ to be our teacher. We immerse ourselves in his life, allow his words to shape us inwardly, and live out of his revelation as faithfully as we can.

This adventure will seldom be straightforward or neat and tidy. Discipleship, like life, can be messy, complex, and difficult. Nonetheless, as we yoke ourselves to Jesus in the way described above, we do begin to live differently. We find ourselves living with different attitudes, different words, and different behaviors. Over time we sense that we are becoming new people, developing Christlike habits and Christlike responses that become part of our nature, which we don't have to think too much about. Amazingly, we learn from our experience that Christ can be our living teacher, just as he was for Mary on that first Easter morning.

If you really want to become a learner of Jesus, may I invite you into this experiment: Set aside a few months to read one of the Gospels slowly and thoroughly. Perhaps you could start with the Gospel of Mark. Soak yourself in those words the Gospel writer gives as coming from Jesus himself. Let his words form you, shape you, challenge you. Let the phrases sink deeply into your heart and mind. Don't rush the process by telling yourself that you have read all these words before. Take time to pray in order to incorpo-

Ask the Lord to make his word
and his Spirit come alive in your heart,
so that you may see your daily life
through God's eyes.

rate what you learn into your place of work, your home, your relationships, and your hopes for the future. Ask the Lord to make his word and his Spirit come alive in your heart, so that you may see your daily life through God's eyes, lit with the light of the word that God has spoken to you.

As you go about this immersion of yourself in Mark's Gospel, learn to live your life as Christ would if he were in your place. Seek the help and power of God's Spirit. Improvise, with the help of others, a life of faith, hope, and compassionate caring in your relationships, in your work, and in your town. In time you will sense God changing you from the inside out, helping you respond to the conditions of your life differently. Remember, you will gradually find yourself living with different habits, attitudes, words, and behaviors. You will also discover—and this is an amazing gift of grace—that you are not alone. Jesus, in the power of his Spirit, steps out of the pages of the Gospel and becomes an empowering presence and close companion in the daily experience of your life.

Follow Mary's example and become a learner of Jesus. You will discover life at its best!

Memory Verse

Take my yoke upon you and learn from me, for I am gentle and humble in heart, and you will find rest for your souls.
—Matthew 11:29

Breath Prayer

Lord, teach me how to be your disciple.

Time to Reflect

Describe the thoughts and feelings you experienced while reading this chapter.

Taking It Further in Group Sharing

- Describe the influence of one significant person upon your life.

- In what ways has Christ been your living teacher?

- In what specific area of your present life experience do you need Christ's guidance?

Chapter 7

LETTING GO
AND LETTING GOD

Jesus said, "Do not hold on to me. . . ."

—John 20:17

There is a story of a man who was climbing a mountain when he lost his balance and fell. Just as he was going over the edge of the cliff, he grabbed hold of a small branch and held on for dear life. Swinging there over the abyss, he prayed, "O God, help me."

A gentle voice answered, "Do you trust me?"

"You know I trust you, Lord; that's why I'm speaking to you."

The voice asked again, "Do you trust me?"

"Yes, Lord, of course I trust you."

This time the voice came back loudly, "Then let go."

A different ending to the story notes the man asking, "Is there anyone else up there I can speak to?"

Seriously though, if we want to experience God's peace and power at a deeper level, we need to learn to let go. This does not mean becoming passive or inactive or irresponsible. Nor does it mean saying "what will be will be" in a spirit of resignation. Letting go is an act of true surrender. No longer do we insist on having everything go our way. We let go of the *I*, *me*, and *mine*. We give up sitting on the throne of our life and allow Christ to become our Lord. We align our will with God's viewpoint and begin seeking God's way for our everyday life. Taking the risk of letting go, of entrusting ourselves to God, lies at the heart of personal transformation. The more we trust, the more we let God be God, the freer we become.

I believe this truth is what Mary Magdalene began to discover on that resurrection morning. Go back for a moment to those words that Jesus spoke to her, "Don't hold onto me." At first glance they seem a little uncaring. They must surely have pierced her heart. The past two nights had probably been the darkest period of her life. She had gone through heartache and desolation. She thought she would never see Jesus again or hear his voice or feel his touch. As she recognized him in this moment and realized that he was alive, we can understand her instinctive

Taking the risk of letting go, of entrusting ourselves to God, lies at the heart of personal transformation.

desire to throw her arms around him, to never let go of him again. Yet Jesus does not want her to do this.

In reality, Jesus is not being insensitive. He is inviting Mary to enter a new level in their relationship. Jesus, the one who comforts, now becomes the one who challenges. His command is crisp and clear. He asks Mary not to cling to him. He wants her to learn to let go and let God. To open her hands and trust.

Jesus has deeper intentions for Mary's life. He does not want her to remain a clinger all her life. He knows that clinging shrinks the soul, undermines trust, and impedes the growth of a transforming friendship with God. And so he yearns for her to open her clenched fists and to become a person who is able to let go. If she really desires to continue her journey toward transformation, she must be set

Conversion is a lifelong process that takes place gradually, one day at a time.

free from the need to cling and learn to let go. And so he commands her, "Don't hold onto me." It's the invitation of love, the challenge of radical trust that asks for open hands.

People who belong to Alcoholics Anonymous express perfectly what Jesus is asking Mary to do in this passage. They speak of how important it is "to let go and let God." This slogan underlines how vital it is to surrender all of our certainties, to entrust ourselves completely to God, to be willing to let God be God in our lives. From personal experience Jesus knows the peace and power that comes when we do this. Hours before his crucifixion, he prayed in Gethsemane the prayer of someone who knew what it meant to let go: "Father, not my will but yours be done." Jesus wants Mary to enter into that same deep experience of trusting, surrender, and letting go.

The decision to let go and let God is not something we do once and for all. Our initial surrender to Christ allows him, as it were, entrance through the front door of our house. It expresses our willingness to let God transform, if necessary, the whole of our personal, sexual, financial, and social lives. But it is only the beginning of the faith journey. In order to live fully in the house of transformation, we need to turn over to Christ, room by room, every aspect of our personalities, especially those rooms hidden from public view. As we do this, we learn that conversion is a lifelong process that takes place gradually, one day at a time.

I need to emphasize that this process of letting go can be a real struggle. The part of us that wants to be at the center, to be in control, to have life work out "our way," constantly tries to get back on the throne of our lives. We can surrender our whole lives to God first thing in the morning. But an hour later we can find ourselves sick with worry about some aspect of our work or about our finances or about the future of our country. We can entrust our loved ones to God and pray that they will become all that God wants them to be. But within minutes we may find ourselves telling them how they should be running their lives. As we catch ourselves doing this, all we can do is to return gently to Christ, express again our willingness to let go and to let God, and ask God to continue to guide us as the day goes along.

As you end this meditation, I invite you to share in a brief exercise, one that I do again and again. Wherever you may be sitting now, make yourself comfortable and place your hands upon your lap. Curl up your fingers into tightly closed fists. Imagine that in these tightly clenched hands you are holding on to everything that is important for you— your life, your loved ones, your work, your possessions, your resentments, your hopes and dreams for the future. Feel the tension build up from your hands. Now hear Christ's invitation to let go and let God. It is an invitation to deeper surrender and yieldedness. As you are able, allow your response to find expression in the slow opening of your hands.

May you know the joy and serenity that come from letting go and letting God!

Memory Verse

"Father, into your hands I commit my spirit."

—Luke 23:46

Breath Prayer

Lord, help me live with open hands.

Time to Reflect

Describe the thoughts and feelings you experienced while reading this chapter.

Taking It Further in Group Sharing

- How do you respond to the word *surrender*?

- What has helped you to deepen your trust in God?

- How are you needing to "let go and let God" at the moment?

Chapter 8

GIVING SPACE
TO LOVED ONES

Jesus said, "Do not hold on to me, for I have not yet ascended to the Father."

—John 20:17

A few months ago, I watched my eighteen-year-old daughter walk away from me through the departure lounge of the Johannesburg Airport. She was on her way to board a plane bound for London. She had been planning this trip for several years and had saved every cent she could. It was going to be a two-month holiday during which she hoped to listen to her favorite punk bands, visit some art galleries, and experience life in another country.

It was also her first time away from home for any length of time.

As she turned to wave good-bye, I felt conflicting emotions. On the one hand, I was happy for her. She was growing up, leaving behind her childhood dependencies, and beginning to explore life on her own. I wanted her to know that she was going with my full blessing. In spoken and unspoken ways in the days prior to her leaving, I had tried to convey the message, "I love you; I trust you; I am proud of you and send you off freely. You are my deeply beloved daughter, and I delight in you."

But on the other hand, I was not finding it easy to let go. While I knew with my head the importance of allowing her freedom, a part of me still longed for those days when she would sit on my lap and uncritically take in everything I said. Those times, however, were long gone. I knew that the time had come to put behind me the way we used to relate to each other. I realized that I needed to learn to connect with my daughter in a new way that would give her space and freedom to become the person she wanted to be.

The widely read spiritual writer Henri J. M. Nouwen has pointed out that real intimacy involves both closeness and distance. Finding the balance, however, can be difficult. Sometimes we need to be held and hugged. At other times we need the space to move freely. What makes matters even trickier is that the needs of the two people

If we honestly try to discern when to come close or when to allow space, it can often open up our closest relationships to new growth and much deeper intimacy.

in a relationship usually differ at any given moment. One person may need closeness while the other wants distance. One might want to be held while the other needs space. In spite of these difficulties, if we honestly try to discern when to come close or when to allow space, it can often open up our closest relationships to new growth and much deeper intimacy.

It seems that Mary Magdalene was the kind of person who found it easier to hold on to loved ones than to give them space. So Jesus wants her now to open herself to a new spacious intimacy in their relationship. He encourages her in this direction by assuring her that, as the ascended Lord, his spiritual presence will be present throughout the universe. Wherever Mary goes, whatever she does, he will be with her. Nothing will ever separate

God always offers the gift of personal love
freely, and we are free
to respond in our own way.

her from his resurrection love and presence. Therefore she must not cling to him. "Do not hold on to me," he says to her, "for I have not yet ascended to the Father."

Perhaps we also find it difficult to give space to our loved ones. Often in our close relationships we try to possess and hold on to one another. We do this because we need security or because it gives us a false sense that we are in control and in charge of what happens. It could also be that our need to be loved has become so great that when someone does show us some affection and caring, we are inclined to cling to them. We demand more from them than they are able to give. As a result, many people feel suffocated in their relationships, as if they are not being given enough freedom to breathe, to live, and to move. As someone said to me in a marriage-counseling interview recently, "I just need some space to be my own person."

God's relationship with each of us gives us a remarkable model of spacious intimacy. Have you ever noticed that God is seldom pushy? I cannot speak for you, but I have never experienced the divine presence forcing itself on me. Nor have I ever known God to coerce or pressure me into a particular course of action. God always offers the gift of personal love freely, and we are free to respond in our own way. Similarly, the Spirit normally moves in our hearts and minds in a quiet, gentle, and inviting way. It never forces its will on us. For this reason we are often able to avoid or explain away God's loving overtures toward us. And when we do, God rarely responds with fire from heaven. More likely, God simply gives us the space to continue our lives as we choose.

In the same way that God relates to us, we need to relate to others. On the one hand, we really want to be able to express our love and care for them. On the other hand, we should do so without holding on to them. We need to learn how to take our hands off of their lives. In this way we give our loved ones space. When we let them go in this way, we are making a statement like this:

> "I believe that you were created to live freely. I place your life into the loving hands of your Creator. I let go of my clinging hold on your life. I am willing for you to make your own choices. I no longer want to play god in your life. I will not believe that I always know what is best for your life. I want you to live your life according to your best understanding and light. I respect the image of God in you. I want to learn to love you with open hands. I love you, and I bless you. I have confidence in you and always will."

Right now, you may want to say these words aloud on behalf of a particular loved one you would like to think about. This person may be struggling with alcohol or substance abuse or making choices with which you disagree or refusing to respond to your gestures of love and affection in the way you would like. Notice how these affirmations affect your interactions with this person. Wait on God and see how God's Spirit works in your relationship. You may find yourself surprised by a little Easter. Any time we experience new possibilities for life and healing in our close relationships, a little Easter occurs—offering a glimpse of the power of resurrection love. May this experience be yours in the days ahead.

Memory Verse

Greater love has no one than this: to lay down one's life for one's friends.

—John 15:13

Breath Prayer

Lord, I place my loved ones in your hands.

Time to Reflect

Describe the thoughts and feelings you experienced while reading this chapter.

Taking It Further in Group Sharing

- Describe a time when you needed to give space to a loved one.

- What helps you give space to loved ones?

- How do you sense God calling you at the moment to deeper intimacy in your close relationships?

Chapter 9

SHARING THE MESSAGE

"Go instead to my brothers and tell them, 'I am ascending to my Father and your Father, to my God and your God.'" Mary Magdalene went to the disciples with the news: "I have seen the Lord!" And she told them that he had said these things to her.

—John 20:17–18

Over the past few years I have learned a great deal from my friends who attend Alcoholics Anonymous. They often tell me about the 12-step program that they are seeking to follow. Few other programs have brought as much healing and transformation into people's lives as this one. Built into this life-saving program is the necessity to pass on the message of hope and recovery to others. The twelfth step reads, "Having had a spiritual awakening as a result of these steps, we try to carry this message to others and to practice these principles in all our affairs." Implied in this step is the belief that, in order for recovering alcoholics to stay on the road to recovery, they must share what they have received.

I believe that this principle also holds true for those who want to follow Christ. We need to pass on the good news that has touched our lives. When we do so, our faith continues to grow and deepen. When we don't, our faith often shrivels up and dies. This could be why my prayer counselor, on the night of my first public commitment to Jesus, insisted, "Trevor, please make sure that you tell someone as soon as you can about the step that you have taken tonight." He must have known that sharing Christ with others makes him more real to us as well.

But we don't share our faith only because it keeps us spiritually alive. We share our faith because Jesus insists that we do so. We see this requirement clearly in the final moments of his encounter with Mary Magdalene. Their time together comes to an end with Jesus challenging Mary to go and share the news of his resurrection with his disciples. Still living in the darkness of Good Friday, they need to receive the wonderful news of resurrection hope and light. Jesus knows this, and he wants Mary to be the bearer of this message.

Mary responds immediately. She runs to the disciples and tells them, "I have seen the Lord!" Notice that she does not tell the disciples what they ought to believe or to do.

We need to pass on the good news that has touched our lives. When we do so, our faith continues to grow and deepen.

Nor does she engage in any kind of theological argument or discussion. She simply tells her story. She has personally seen Jesus with the eyes of faith and knows that his living presence will always be with her. The power of the resurrection begins to flow through her to others. She becomes an Easter person living in a Good Friday world.

The Living One continues to call you and me to be Easter people in a Good Friday world. As he did with Mary, Jesus calls us to go to the dark places of our world, which are marked by the signs of crucifixion. He calls us to where our neighbors and friends live in the darkness of despair and loneliness. He calls us into those communities where poverty, homelessness, and crime block out the sunlight. He calls us to descend into those dark pits where people feel cut off and abandoned by God. In all these dark places, his challenge remains the same. We must listen to the stories of those who suffer. Wipe away the tears. Share with others our personal experience of the Easter message.

How do we pass on this Easter message? Certainly not by trying to force others to believe exactly the same way that we do. Nor by attempting to "fix" those around us with our solutions and prescriptions for their lives. Mary teaches us that the best way to be a witness is by sharing our personal story; by telling others how the living Christ has shone the light in our darkness; by explaining the difference that letting go and letting God has made to our lives; by testifying how our lives have been touched by resurrection love; and to always do this with gentleness, respect, and courtesy. I think it was D. T. Niles who once said that passing on the good news is like "one beggar telling another beggar where he or she can find some bread."

Usually the opportunities to share our personal experiences of God come only after we have tried to get to know people on their own terms. This means expressing interest in them and what they are going through instead of trying to look for gaps to speak about our spiritual pilgrimage. I am aware that this may sound contradictory to the usual ideas associated with "spreading the word." But I

We must listen to the stories of those who suffer.

have learned over the years that our best witness to God's personal love consists of keeping quiet and listening before we talk. When we listen before we speak, we get a much better hearing from others.

If you want to experiment with my suggestion, go from reading this passage and ask someone with whom you either live or work how he or she is doing. Listen and show an active interest in the response. I'm sure the person will sense a change in you and want to know why!

A recent conversation brought home for me again the importance of being interested in others if we want to bear witness for Christ. At a wedding reception I was seated alongside a rather impressive-looking man. We introduced ourselves, and I learned that he was a doctor working in the same city where I worked. He asked me what I did for

I have learned over the years that our best witness to God's personal love consists of keeping quiet and listening before we talk.

a living. I told him that I was a pastor of a local congregation. When he heard this he told me that he was not a religious man, did not go to church, and no longer believed in God. I was genuinely intrigued by what he said and tried to show my interest.

"Can you tell me about this God in whom you don't believe?" I inquired.

"Certainly," he answered. "I don't believe at all in a God who sits somewhere up in the sky and controls everything that happens like a puppet master."

"That's interesting," I replied. "Neither do I."

"What kind of God do you believe in?" he asked.

What followed was an exceptionally meaningful conversation. Not only did I learn more about where this man's notions about God had come from, but he also shared at length his previous experiences with the church, some of which had been quite painful. In response to his interest, I was able to share that for me God was not some distant figure but rather a living and active presence with, within, and around me. I told him briefly about some of the strengthening effects that my relationship with God had brought into my life, especially in times of struggle and difficulty. I wish I could say that our conversation had ended with him asking me how to get to know God, but it didn't. His last words to me were, "Well, you never know; you may see me in church one of these days."

You may be wondering at this point just what you would say if the opportunity arose for you to share your experience of God. Perhaps I could ask you to engage in a simple exercise that may help you to find the words to tell your own faith story. Begin by thinking about a real-life problem that you have had to deal with recently in some area of your life. It may have been a difficulty in your marriage, a crisis at work, a financial struggle, a battle with depression, or another personal experience. Ask yourself how your relationship with the risen Christ made a difference in how you responded to this problem. Write down your response.

When you have completed the exercise, you have the beginnings of your own up-to-date Easter story at hand, ready to be shared.

Memory Verse

But you will receive power when the Holy Spirit comes on you; and you will be my witnesses.

—Acts 1:8

Breath Prayer

Lord, help me be your witness today.

Time to Reflect

Describe the thoughts and feelings you experienced while reading this chapter.

Taking It Further in Group Sharing

- Who was the first person to share the message of Christ with you?

- How do you feel talking about your faith?

- Share a recent experience where the risen Christ helped you face a difficult problem.

Chapter 10

EXPLORING OUR
LIVING HOPE

Praise be to the God and Father of our Lord Jesus Christ! In his great mercy he has given us a new birth into a living hope through the resurrection of Jesus Christ from the dead.

—1 Peter 1:3

L et me be open and honest with you. I have deeply conflicting reactions to death. A huge part of me really loves life and enjoys the good things of this physical world and wants to delay my departure from it for as long as possible. This part of me does not enjoy thinking about death, especially my own or the death of those close to me.

The death of my father some years ago left a lot of pain in my heart that continues until today.

Another part of me *does* want to face the issue of death and think seriously about its consequences. As I get older I find my thoughts drawn to the subject more and more. What will it be like? What lies beyond? How can I face it with dignity and without fear? Will I be able to recognize those whom I have loved? The questions go on and on.

However, I have found that there are not many people with whom I can honestly share my feelings about death. Death is a subject most people want to avoid. Our generation fears many things, but it fears few things more than it does death. Can you imagine, the next time you attend a dinner party or share a meal with your friends at a restaurant, asking those you are with, "What do you feel and think about death?" Your question will probably generate a fair degree of discomfort and unease. A real wet blanket!

One reason for this avoidance is the strongly materialistic outlook of our day and age. Our lives have been powerfully shaped by a culture that focuses on the physical. We are strongly tempted to believe that the only things that are real in life are those things that we can taste and see and smell and touch. Therefore, when we consider the possibility of our bodies decomposing when we die, there is a deep-rooted feeling that this actually could be the end of our existence.

How incredibly different must Mary Magdalene's attitude toward death have been after her encounter with

We are strongly tempted to believe that the only things that are real in life are those things that we can taste and see and smell and touch.

the risen Christ. On that first Easter morning—when she found the tomb empty, heard her name being called, and discovered that Jesus was alive—her heart must have been filled with an amazing sense of hope. The love that Jesus had shown her, the love that he had lived, the love that he embodied had not been defeated by the dark power of death. I can almost picture her running back to the disciples with a new song in her heart. Death was not the end.

Jesus, her Lord, was alive again, living beyond a terrible crucifixion in a completely new and transformed way!

And how do you think the disciples responded when Mary arrived at their door with the news, "I have seen the Lord"? Did they smile knowingly, thinking to themselves that she may have cracked under the pressure? Did they won-

❧

[The Christ-followers] knew that their death was a doorway into a new dimension of life in an eternal kingdom. They knew they were safe.

❧

der whether she was hallucinating? Or did they look at each other with the subtle fear that sometimes comes to us in those moments when we become aware that the world is not as we think it is? Whatever their reaction may have been, it probably did not bother Mary too much. She had personally experienced the living presence of Jesus. She knew that there was now nothing left to fear, not even the terrible reality of death.

As followers of Jesus we are invited to share in Mary's living hope and allow "resurrection possibilities" into our dark situations. For example, through the centuries the attitude of Christ-followers toward death has been in marked contrast to the attitudes of others around them. Remember how the early Christian martyrs went to their deaths in the Coliseum singing and praising, even blessing those who had sentenced them to death. They were not playacting. They were living out of their confident assurance that their relationship with Christ, begun in this life, would continue in an ever richer and fuller way. They knew that their death was a doorway into a new dimension of life in an eternal kingdom. They knew they were safe.

Having a living hope does not mean that we have unrealistic attitudes toward trouble and suffering or that we do not experience deep grief when a loved one dies. Of course we feel grief and the awful pain and anguish that comes when we can no longer touch someone we have loved deeply. We cry; we grieve; we hurt like anyone else. Sometimes we might even shake our fists at God, wondering how this could have been allowed to happen—especially when we lose a child. And if we have built our lives and our hopes entirely on our loved ones, then our joy will always be a fragile thing. But if our deepest confidence resides in the God who raised Jesus from the dead, then our sadness will not be trapped in hopelessness and despair. We will be able to grieve with hope.

We can shape our lives and actions
to reflect the pattern of Jesus'
unconditional love for us.

Can you see now why the most important challenge we face in this life is to grow our relationship with the risen Christ and the God whom he reveals? Nothing is more important. The practical aspects of how we do this is not the central theme of this book, but let me briefly note a few things that have helped me on my pilgrimage:

- We can think deeply about the resurrection narratives of Jesus. These stories remind us that the final word about our lives belongs to God and not death. They help us to see that there is far more to this universe than what meets the eye.

- We can get to know all we can about Jesus of Nazareth by reading and rereading the four Gospels. Once our lives have been touched by his resurrected presence, he becomes the Way, the Truth, and the Life for us. As we learn to follow him, he steps out of the Gospel and becomes a living presence for us.

- We can share regularly together with other worshipers in Holy Communion. As we take the broken bread and drink the wine, the risen Lord renews our faith and our hope in him.

- We can shape our lives and actions to reflect the pattern of Jesus' unconditional love for us. This always serves as the acid test of whether our lives have been touched by the living Jesus or not: are we growing in our ability to love the people around us in the same way that Christ has loved us?

- We can keep our hope alive in all the situations we face, even death and dying. This hope will take decision and determination. We must courageously turn our faces away from worry, fear, and cynicism and choose to be people of hope. As we consciously lean on our risen Lord and Friend in tough situations, we will be given the inner resources to face life in amazing ways.

In closing—Mary's encounter with the risen Jesus on that first Easter morning shows us how his resurrection can give birth to a living hope in our lives, a living hope that our pools of tears will actually become opportunities for transformation and growth, a living hope that reminds us that at the heart of all things stands a resurrection love that will never let us go. Above all, it is a living hope that even death cannot take away and that enables us to cry out with all those who have gone before us, "Where, O death, is your victory? Where, O death, is your sting?" (1 Cor. 15:55).

Memory Verse

Be joyful in hope, patient in affliction, faithful in prayer.

—Romans 12:12

Breath Prayer

Lord, be my living hope today.

Time to Reflect

Describe the thoughts and feelings you experienced while reading this chapter.

Taking It Further in Group Sharing

- What are your thoughts and feelings about death and dying?

- What role does hope play in your life?

- How can you practically deepen your relationship with the risen Christ?

AN OUTLINE FOR
SMALL-GROUP USE

Here is a simple plan for a one-hour, weekly group discussion. One person may act as convener every week, or the role can rotate among group members. You may choose to light a white Christ candle each week to signal the beginning of your time together.

Opening

Convener: Let us come into the presence of God.

Others: Lord Jesus Christ, thank you for being with us. May we hear your word to us as we speak to one another.

Discussion

Convener asks others to share their impressions of the chapter assigned for the week. Use the questions for group discussion at the end of each chapter (reprinted below) as a guide to the discussion.

Chapter 1

- In what ways can you identify with Mary as she stands weeping outside the tomb?

- What would it mean for you to look up to God through your tears and hope for new beginnings?

- How does the message of Jesus' death and resurrection help you to befriend your tears?

Chapter 2

- Describe a time in your life when someone was there for you in a time of struggle and pain.

- What did this person teach you about being a wailing wall for others?

- What or who helps you to process pain in your life?

Chapter 3

- Share one experience where you felt God used you to "weep with those who weep."? (Be careful not to mention the names of the people involved.)

- What was this experience like for you?

- What human cry in your surrounding community moves you most deeply at the moment?

Chapter 4

- How do you respond to the archbishop's words about God's personal love for each one of us?
- Describe a time when God's love touched you in a special way.
- How do you experience God's love in your daily life?

Chapter 5

- Describe your first "turning moment."
- How do you experience God during your turning moments?
- In what ways do you sense God nudging you into a deeper repentance?

Chapter 6

- Describe the influence of one significant person upon your life.
- In what ways has Christ been your living teacher?

- In what specific area of your present life experience do you need Christ's guidance?

Chapter 7

- How do you respond to the word *surrender*?
- What has helped you to deepen your trust in God?
- How are you needing to "let go and let God" at the moment?

Chapter 8

- Describe a time when you needed to give space to a loved one.
- What helps you give space to loved ones?
- How do you sense God calling you at the moment to deepen the intimacy in your close relationships?

Chapter 9

- Who was the first person to share the message of Christ with you?
- How do you feel talking about your faith?

- Share a recent experience where the risen Christ helped you face a difficult problem.

Chapter 10

- What are your thoughts and feelings about death and dying?

- What role does hope play in your life?

- How can you practically deepen your relationship with the risen Christ?

Praying Together

Convener says: Based on today's discussion, what people and situations do you want us to pray for now and in the coming week?

Convener or other volunteer then prays about the concerns named.

Departing

Convener says: Let us go in peace to serve God and our neighbors in all that we do.

Adapted from *The Upper Room* daily devotional guide, January-February 2001. © 2000 The Upper Room. Used by permission.

ACKNOWLEDGMENTS

I want to express my deep gratitude to the folk at Upper Room Books for their willingness to publish *Hope beyond Your Tears* for an overseas readership. It is a book very close to my heart, and I am delighted that it will be available more widely. Thank-you to Jeannie Crawford-Lee, Eli Fisher, Rita Collett, and their team for all that they have done to make this happen.

Thank-you to fellow pilgrim Bill Meaker for his patient reading of each chapter and his helpful comments.

It is an honor to have Dallas Willard write the Foreword. Over the years, his friendship and his writings have profoundly shaped my understanding of what it means to follow Jesus.

How do I say thank-you to Debbie, my partner in marriage, to our children Joni and Mark? Our life together is the greatest gift I have been given. God is indeed good, gracious, and generous.

Finally, I thank the risen Lord for his faithful companionship in each moment of my life. I ask that he will use these words to help others find hope beyond their tears.

—*Trevor Hudson, 2012*

ALSO BY TREVOR HUDSON

The Serenity Prayer
A Simple Prayer to Enrich Your Life
Peace. We all want it, but often it gets drowned out by the everyday struggles of life. If you've dealt with inner discontent, restlessness, anxiety, stress, guilt, grief, pain in relationships, or just everyday pressures, *The Serenity Prayer* offers a profound look into a simple prayer that will deepen your trust and reliance on God.

Paperback • 978-0-8358-1094-4 • 128 pages

One Day at a Time
Discovering the Freedom of 12-Step Spirituality
Addiction, personal weakness, and feelings of inadequacy are issues many people face daily. Using a step-by-step plan for a lifetime commitment to change, Hudson offers principles that will help you learn to reclaim a sense of self-worth and renewal in your life.

Paperback • 978-0-8358-9913-0 • 160 pages

Questions God Asks Us

Trevor Hudson will captivate you with his invitation to consider 10 questions God asks us. Rather than finding fault or putting you on the spot, Hudson reveals questions that lead to a deep dialogue between you and God.

Paperback • 978-0-8358-9990-1 • 144 pages

The Way of Transforming Discipleship
A Companions in Christ resource
Trevor Hudson and Stephen D. Bryant

Trevor Hudson is one of the leading voices of reconciliation in the South African Christian community. In *The Way of Transforming Discipleship*, he shares lessons that will help Christians everywhere become agents of truth-telling and reconciliation. This five-week resource is ideal for small-group studies, Lenten studies, or preparation for mission trips.

Participant's Book
Paperback • 978-0-8358-9842-3 • 96 pages

Leader's Guide by Stephen D. Bryant
Paperback • 978-0-8358-9841-6 • 96 pages

A Mile in My Shoes
Cultivating Compassion

Many think of a pilgrimage as a long journey that must be taken in a foreign land. However, *A Mile in My Shoes* helps us discover the possibilities of being on a pilgrimage in our own communities. Hudson enables us to benefit richly from his experience in South Africa and apply it to our own personal and community circumstances.

7 weeks • Includes Reflection Questions

Paperback • 978-0-8358-9815-7 • 128 pages

Listening to the Groans
A Spirituality for Ministry and Mission

Trevor Hudson and Stephen D. Bryant

In this short but powerful book, Hudson and Bryant call you to reject spirituality that is only inward, personal, and individual and to pray your way toward a broader understanding of the Spirit. They challenge you to listen for those moments when "the world groans in pain and hope" and to respond with both prayer and action in faithful and compassionate living. An excellent companion or follow-up to *The Way of Transforming Discipleship*.

Paperback • 978-0-8358-9933-8 • 64 pages